TO: _____

FROM: _____

Things You Can Save

WHEN YOU LOSE
SOMEONE
CLOSE TO YOUR HEART

by Benecia Aronwald
illustrated by Jill Weber

LIFE FAVORS™
Random House 🏠 New York

When you lose someone
close to your heart

there are things you can do
to keep your memories alive

There are things you can save

Something you can put

in your pocket

Or wear

in a locket

Something you can

put in a box

Take on a walk

Or keep with

your socks

Something that

Protect you

from the storm

Something that makes you feel good

when you wear it

Makes you feel confident

makes you feel strong

Makes you feel
they are still
with you...

Beside you

Looking over
or after you

Helping to

guide you

Making you feel

Loved